© **SALES MANTRAS**
BY SANDEEP RAVIDUTT SHARMA

Table of Contents

Introduction IV

Sales Mantras...1

© SALES MANTRAS
BY SANDEEP RAVIDUTT SHARMA

Introduction

This book provides with **100 random sales tips and quotes for the sales guy** focussing mainly on building a healthy customer-centric business. Accumulating knowledge is fine, but applying it in real life situation is desirable. Not everyone is able to sell effectively due to various reasons. The first and foremost reason is that the salesperson often forgets that it is the customer who rules. The products are made for the customer and not for self-consumption. The positive attitude of the salesperson and proper understanding of the customer requirement goes a long way to create a win-win situation. This book is just a small attempt to share or remind the interested ones about the basic rules and process that one should follow when it's a matter of selling products and solutions.

I'm sure if you keep reading, referring, sharing these quotes, you may derive inspiration and develop a good understanding of various business perspectives and facts. I sincerely hope, you will find this book amazing, interesting, rejuvenating, unique and a constant source of inspiration.

Thank You and Happy Reading.

© SALES MANTRAS
BY SANDEEP RAVIDUTT SHARMA

© **Copyright 2018 Sandeep Ravidutt Sharma - All rights reserved.**
In no way is it legal to reproduce, duplicate, or transmit any part of this document in either electronic means or in printed format. Recording of this publication is strictly prohibited and any storage of this document is not allowed unless with written permission from the publisher. All rights reserved. The information provided herein is stated to be truthful and consistent, in that any liability, in terms of inattention or otherwise, by any usage or abuse of any policies, processes, or directions contained within is the solitary and utter responsibility of the recipient reader. Under no circumstances will any legal responsibility or blame be held against the author / publisher for any reparation, damages, or monetary loss due to the information herein, either directly or indirectly. The author own all copyrights.

Legal Notice:
This book is copyright protected. This is only for personal use. You cannot amend, distribute, sell, use, quote or paraphrase any part or the content within this book without the consent of the author or copyright owner. Legal action will be pursued if this is breached.

Disclaimer Notice:
Please note the information contained within this book is for motivational, educational and knowledge sharing purpose only. Every attempt has been made to provide the reader accurate, up to date and reliable complete information. No warranties of any kind are expressed or implied. Readers acknowledge that the author is not engaging in the rendering of legal, financial, medical or professional advice. By reading this document, the reader agrees that under no circumstances the author / publisher is responsible for any losses, direct or indirect, which are incurred as a result of the use of information contained within this document, including, but not limited to, —errors, omissions, or inaccuracies.

If you have further questions, contact on
Tel: +919969256731
Email: sandeepraviduttsharma@gmail.com

© SALES MANTRAS
BY SANDEEP RAVIDUTT SHARMA

Dedication

This book is dedicated to **Goddess Bhairavi**. In the Hindu religion, the Goddess Bhairavi represents divine anger and wrath which is directed towards impurities within us as well as to the negative forces that obstructs our spiritual growth. Bhairavi Mata is also called as **Shubhamkari** and does good things. She is often depicted in images as holding a book, rosary and making abhaya and varada mudra with her hands. She is fiercely protective, lending us wisdom and power, steadiness and clarity. She personifies light and fire, supporting us to reveal what we keep hidden and inviting us to explore our hidden mind and any secret darkness.

I hereby recite the following Bhairavi mool mantra...
"Om Hreem Bhairavi Kalaum Hreem Svaha"
And pray to **Goddess Bhairavi** for lending wisdom and power, steadiness and clarity in the life of my readers and the world. May Goddess Bhairavi protect us from negative forces along with removing impurities of our mind.

SALES MANTRAS

© SALES MANTRAS
BY SANDEEP RAVIDUTT SHARMA

The first impression creates a lasting impact on your customer. Welcome the customer with a smile. Introduce yourself and your company in the best way you know before starting to sell. A good first impression is your best chance to successful selling. Make use of this opportunity in the best possible way.

© SALES MANTRAS
BY SANDEEP RAVIDUTT SHARMA

The positive impression and suggestions often helps the salesperson to build a good rapport with the customer and ultimately leads to closing the deal. Those who are able to strike a common chord with the customer in the first few minutes of the conversation can hope to make a sale.

© SALES MANTRAS
BY SANDEEP RAVIDUTT SHARMA

Customers like to negotiate with the salesperson to arrive at the best deal. Negotiate wisely. First try to know the perspective of the customer, ask for more if you expect the customer to bring down the offer price, agree for a price which is a win-win proposition for both.

© **SALES MANTRAS**
BY SANDEEP RAVIDUTT SHARMA

Accumulating knowledge is fine but applying it in real life situation is desirable. Be ready to know more about what it would take to make a sale. Make use of your knowledge to understand the requirements of the customer well so as to suggest the best product available.

© **SALES MANTRAS**
BY SANDEEP RAVIDUTT SHARMA

Keep talking to your sales team and do a review of the customer's response. Study the response with a positive approach and be ready with your action plan to take the next step forward to make a sale.

© SALES MANTRAS
BY SANDEEP RAVIDUTT SHARMA

Even your best product needs effective selling. Never take any sales call lightly. In this competitive world and information age, the customer mostly calls the shot. Be ready to convince the customer about why your product is the best. Simply ignore talking about how the rival product scores less than your product. Speak about how your product suits your customers requirement well.

© **SALES MANTRAS**
BY SANDEEP RAVIDUTT SHARMA

Successful sales person always looks ahead of his individual target. Do not just sell a product because you want to achieve your target. Sell it because you want to help the customer meet his needs and in the process you achieve your self target.

© SALES MANTRAS
BY SANDEEP RAVIDUTT SHARMA

Be a good listener and kindly allow the customer to speak out what he wants. Listening always helps whether it is a matter of sales or your life in general. When you listen carefully, you are able to understand things wide and clear about what the customer wants. Also, listening helps you to selectively provide information which the customer is seeking and not serve junk.

© SALES MANTRAS
BY SANDEEP RAVIDUTT SHARMA

Successful salesperson first demonstrates the product effectively before prompting the customer to close the deal. Demonstration of the product features is more important than just negotiating the price. Once the customer is convinced about the product features and how it resolves his problem, the prices becomes secondary for him.

© SALES MANTRAS
BY SANDEEP RAVIDUTT SHARMA

Gauge the buying capacity of the customer by showing products from a varied price range and not just ask for the budget. The smart salesperson is able to judge the buying capacity of the customer in few minutes without even asking the customer by simply reading the expression and feedback against the products showcased.

© **SALES MANTRAS**
BY SANDEEP RAVIDUTT SHARMA

Be in touch with your customers post-sales, and you are sure to get more sales from them or through their references. Once you struck a deal, ensure that you still follow up with your customer for the feedback about how the product is helping him to address his requirements. A satisfied customer is most likely to give you repeat sales as well as refer your product to his friends and associates.

© SALES MANTRAS
BY SANDEEP RAVIDUTT SHARMA

Always insist on written confirmation or purchase order while closing the deal especially the high-value ones. The written communication is always preferable to just oral talks when you want to close the deal. Insist on written communication about the order which should be equally responded by giving a written quote. Once the customer okays your quote, ask for the signed purchase order.

© **SALES MANTRAS**
BY SANDEEP RAVIDUTT SHARMA

Gather intelligence about the customer so that you can give relevant reference to win the deal.

© SALES MANTRAS
BY SANDEEP RAVIDUTT SHARMA

Your words create an impact, whether it's positive or negative depends on how it was received and interpreted at the other end.

© **SALES MANTRAS**
BY SANDEEP RAVIDUTT SHARMA

Putting efforts to acquire new clients should be the way of life if you want your business to flourish.

© SALES MANTRAS
BY SANDEEP RAVIDUTT SHARMA

A smart salesperson is the one who could sell a chartered plane to a customer who just enquired about the availability of a flight seat. It's all about building a relationship and then convincing the customer to buy what you intend to sell.

© **SALES MANTRAS**
BY SANDEEP RAVIDUTT SHARMA

Cost competitiveness combined with your trustworthy service can win you deals worth millions.

Make use of the best channels of communication to get your word across the potential customer. Once your word has reached, be ready to call and convince the customer about your products and solutions.

© **SALES MANTRAS**
BY SANDEEP RAVIDUTT SHARMA

A smart salesperson is the one who can sell dreams and still get a positive review in the real world.

© SALES MANTRAS
BY SANDEEP RAVIDUTT SHARMA

Acquire newer skills if you want to stay relevant and want prosperity. Selling in the modern world has now become technology driven. Be ready to make the best use of the available technology to reach out and convince the customer.

© SALES MANTRAS
BY SANDEEP RAVIDUTT SHARMA

Nurture your ambitions with a positive attitude not just for a day but for the lifetime. Always wear positive attitude and do the required preparation before you meet your client.

Super successful are those guys who have mastered the art of cloning their success.

© **SALES MANTRAS**
BY SANDEEP RAVIDUTT SHARMA

Most of the customers like to bargain. Help them to arrive at the right price through give and take approach.

© SALES MANTRAS
BY SANDEEP RAVIDUTT SHARMA

Successful selling starts with building a healthy customer relationship on the foundation of trust and respect for each other. Those who are able to get along well with the customer mainly due to their positive attitude and cheerful demeanour are likely to make a sale soon.

© **SALES MANTRAS**
BY SANDEEP RAVIDUTT SHARMA

Effective sellers can revive the dropout clients by addressing their grievance at the earliest and creating a bond of trust for the future.

Be ready to serve instantly to the customer who seems to be in a hurry. Ask for his specific requirement and provide the required product immediately.

© SALES MANTRAS
BY SANDEEP RAVIDUTT SHARMA

Your commitment creates hope and enhances your credibility when you honour in time. Honouring your word is critical to build a healthy business relationship with your client.

© **SALES MANTRAS**
BY SANDEEP RAVIDUTT SHARMA

Earn better returns tomorrow for sure when you have invested your efforts wisely today. Your efforts to find a product meeting the requirement of the customer may fail today, but is sure to attract the customer again due to your sincere efforts put in last time.

© SALES MANTRAS
BY SANDEEP RAVIDUTT SHARMA

Address the customer grievance immediately and resolve it taking your team's support adhering to a time frame. Sometimes the issue may be trivial but not addressed in time by the attending salesperson. It is better to face the customer in order to understand the bone of contention and dissatisfaction. Resolve and you can win the customer back.

© **SALES MANTRAS**
BY SANDEEP RAVIDUTT SHARMA

Excellence exceeds expectations. Be ready to do enough everyday to improve upon your deliverables. With constant improvement and innovation, the day is not far when your excellence will surpass the expectations of others from you.

© SALES MANTRAS
BY SANDEEP RAVIDUTT SHARMA

Never ignore packaging even when you are selling the best product in the market. Those who pay attention to product packaging in addition to making the best quality product always wins.

© SALES MANTRAS
BY SANDEEP RAVIDUTT SHARMA

First, build value then reveal the price to the prospect during your sales conversation.

© SALES MANTRAS
BY SANDEEP RAVIDUTT SHARMA

Forge the bond of friendship leaving aside the doubt and distrust. During your discovery talks with the customer if you are able to find common ground and reach out to a level of comfort and trust, you can sell.

© **SALES MANTRAS**
BY SANDEEP RAVIDUTT SHARMA

Do enough to retain your existing customers, for this sometimes you may also have to slice your profit margin by reducing the offer price.

© **SALES MANTRAS**
BY SANDEEP RAVIDUTT SHARMA

Each customer is different and unique. Change your sales pitch matching the uniqueness of your prospect. A standard sales pitch doesn't alway work, be ready to innovate your talks based on the client response and feedback.

© **SALES MANTRAS**
BY SANDEEP RAVIDUTT SHARMA

Talk about the features and not stress on the price with the customer who is inquiring about buying a Merc.

© SALES MANTRAS
BY SANDEEP RAVIDUTT SHARMA

Ask the right questions to the customer, and you will soon find a way to sell. Your questions very much reveal about the process you follow to deal with a customer. Your questions also creates an impression about your knowledge and experience in front of the customer. Your satisfactory response to the questions can lead to sales. Be ready to fine tune your response to the queries and you can win.

© **SALES MANTRAS**
BY SANDEEP RAVIDUTT SHARMA

Show limited items but relevant ones for the high value customer to arrive at a buying decision soon.

© **SALES MANTRAS**
BY SANDEEP RAVIDUTT SHARMA

Instead of trying to convince the customer, focus on informing about how your products and solutions can address their needs.

Only confidence can sell. The confidence comes from knowledge, experience and interest. If you can talk confidently about providing the best product available to the customer, you can sell.

© **SALES MANTRAS**
BY SANDEEP RAVIDUTT SHARMA

The effective salesperson can make out the decision maker in just one or two calls or meetings. Ask the right questions to gauge the decision making capability of the customer with whom you are dealing with. The moment you find that the person to whom you are talking cannot decide to buy, you need to explore further and convince the person to connect you to the deciding authority.

© **SALES MANTRAS**
BY SANDEEP RAVIDUTT SHARMA

Always read and understand the history of communication with the client before you contact them again. It is always wise to go through the client history before you decide to meet and offer your products to an existing client.

© **SALES MANTRAS**
BY SANDEEP RAVIDUTT SHARMA

Aspirations are fine till the time you have got efforts racing along at the best pace. With dedicated efforts impossible targets sooner or later also becomes achievable.

© SALES MANTRAS
BY SANDEEP RAVIDUTT SHARMA

Instead of trying to put down your competition, it is better to speak about your product strengths.

© **SALES MANTRAS**
BY SANDEEP RAVIDUTT SHARMA

Nothing can hold back a person who is determined and focused.

© **SALES MANTRAS**
BY SANDEEP RAVIDUTT SHARMA

*Be friendly with
your customers but not at
the cost of your competency and
profits.*

If you are a quick thinker and take minimum time to respond effectively, you can do well in sales. Go for it.

Time is never wasted but efforts are. Value efforts not just yours but others as well.

Appreciate the knowledge of the customer about the product and other subjects that became part of the conversation. Appreciation and thankfulness are the keys to win people before you win a deal.

© **SALES MANTRAS**
BY SANDEEP RAVIDUTT SHARMA

Forget about the doubts in case you are learning how to win trust. Give your best to build trust with your customers.

© **SALES MANTRAS**
BY SANDEEP RAVIDUTT SHARMA

If you have proper answers to the customer queries, you move closer to selling. The customers decide to buy many a time just because they got satisfactory reply to their queries.

Avoid overselling if you want repeat business.

Go beyond just giving product information to the customer, first try to understand his requirement and advise on the matching products. Act like a friend or a well wisher to the customer while you recommend the best product which meets the requirement of the customer.

© SALES MANTRAS
BY SANDEEP RAVIDUTT SHARMA

Top sales performer spends more time with the right prospect and is quick to discard the misfits.

© **SALES MANTRAS**
BY SANDEEP RAVIDUTT SHARMA

Ask the right question at the right time to understand what the customer wants. In case of written communication, it is wise to send a set of questions to understand further. In case of oral talks, the questions can be generated instantly based on the live expressions and feedback of the customer to the information offered.

© SALES MANTRAS
BY SANDEEP RAVIDUTT SHARMA

The smart salesperson can make out the buying capacity of the customer through talks, behaviour, and attitude. When you offer the products matching the buying capacity and preferences of the customer, you can sell.

© SALES MANTRAS
BY SANDEEP RAVIDUTT SHARMA

Effectiveness comes from experience and learning attitude. Selling function demands learning at every stage, first starting with the product, company and about the customer. Those who can learn quickly are likely to be successful soon.

Keep your presentation brief and concise. Re-engage prospect during your presentation by asking relevant questions and inviting feedback.

© **SALES MANTRAS**
BY SANDEEP RAVIDUTT SHARMA

Lead the sales process by engaging the customer through your talks about how your product serves his needs.

Offer the solution and not just the product.

© **SALES MANTRAS**
BY SANDEEP RAVIDUTT SHARMA

The customer relies on your expertise to identify products and select the best one satisfying his needs. Expertise comes from product knowledge and capabilities to understand what the customer wants.

© **SALES MANTRAS**
BY SANDEEP RAVIDUTT SHARMA

Success in sales function calls for a higher degree of patience and persistence.

Clearing the inventory during the time of recession at a profit is an acid test for your business. Find innovative ways to do that.

© SALES MANTRAS
BY SANDEEP RAVIDUTT SHARMA

Commit yourself to things or people you like, you will soon find the purpose of your life. If you are in sales, then be ready to commit yourself to building a relationship with the customer, selling the right product which benefits the customer and help you to earn profits for your company. The purpose should be a win-win situation for both and long term relationship.

© **SALES MANTRAS**
BY SANDEEP RAVIDUTT SHARMA

Deal with the intelligent customer with real facts and features. Appreciate the intelligence and knowledge of the customer. Ensure that the customer agrees to the information provided and believes in the factualness and accuracy of the same. You can sell to a customer who is convinced with the facts and figures provided.

© SALES MANTRAS
BY SANDEEP RAVIDUTT SHARMA

Customers choose certain products having sentimental value to them. Respect their sentiments and help them to choose wisely.

A successful sales person is always hopeful of closing the deal.

© **SALES MANTRAS**
BY SANDEEP RAVIDUTT SHARMA

Share relevant intelligence to the customer about how his competitors are making dollars by opting for your solutions.

© SALES MANTRAS
BY SANDEEP RAVIDUTT SHARMA

Your enthusiasm can win a deal. Those who are enthusiastic attracts the attention of the other instantly, the moment you have got the customer's attention, all you have to do is convince him about the usefulness of your product and solutions.

© **SALES MANTRAS**
BY SANDEEP RAVIDUTT SHARMA

Generate more leads by connecting with the right audience.

Good listening skills and a positive attitude can make you a successful sales person.

© SALES MANTRAS
BY SANDEEP RAVIDUTT SHARMA

Those who ensure customer delight are sure to flourish.

© **SALES MANTRAS**
BY SANDEEP RAVIDUTT SHARMA

Gain respect through your actions and not just by your words.

Be ready to share more options with the customer who shows signs of being too choosy and have discarded most of the offerings.

© **SALES MANTRAS**
BY SANDEEP RAVIDUTT SHARMA

Never judge a customer's buying capacity through his attire.

© **SALES MANTRAS**
BY SANDEEP RAVIDUTT SHARMA

Avoid over commitment for closing a sale.

© **SALES MANTRAS**
BY SANDEEP RAVIDUTT SHARMA

Offer discount only when the customer has narrowed down his choice.

© **SALES MANTRAS**
BY SANDEEP RAVIDUTT SHARMA

Look for a unique concept which makes life easy for the customer if you are planning to start a new business.

Progress demands a disciplined approach.

© **SALES MANTRAS**
BY SANDEEP RAVIDUTT SHARMA

Effective sales person never knocks on the customer's door without an appointment.

© **SALES MANTRAS**
BY SANDEEP RAVIDUTT SHARMA

Follow the discipline of the clock when it comes to putting efforts and keep going.

© SALES MANTRAS
BY SANDEEP RAVIDUTT SHARMA

Don't play favourites when you are deputed to chose the best team. Choose people with the right attitude, having the required experience, knows the job and the market well, with high energy levels and full of enthusiasm to achieve the goals set.

Keep your sales presentation brief and concise. Also, ensure zero distraction while you present.

© **SALES MANTRAS**
BY SANDEEP RAVIDUTT SHARMA

Offer alternatives when the price is an issue for the buyer.

© **SALES MANTRAS**
BY SANDEEP RAVIDUTT SHARMA

Let the customer do most of the talking till you know what does he wants to buy.

© SALES MANTRAS
BY SANDEEP RAVIDUTT SHARMA

If you are a trader, buy a product which you can sell to your own self first, before you decide to sell it to your customer.

With the positive mindset and visualisation of closing the deal, you should call your customer.

© **SALES MANTRAS**
BY SANDEEP RAVIDUTT SHARMA

Feed the customer's ego by appreciating his gentlemanly behaviour and known achievements. The customer with a higher self-esteem and who loves appreciation by others is mostly likely to buy your product just to keep his ego atop.

© **SALES MANTRAS**
BY SANDEEP RAVIDUTT SHARMA

Focus on building a relationship based on trust instead of just doing sweet talks.

© SALES MANTRAS
BY SANDEEP RAVIDUTT SHARMA

It's not just your sales pitch that helps you to sell. It is more about your attitude and approach that paves the way for successful selling.

The successful salesperson is the one who always like the challenge and is smart enough to convert them into opportunities.

© SALES MANTRAS
BY SANDEEP RAVIDUTT SHARMA

Smooth collaboration comes from a positive mind.

Aggression is good if it puts you in alert mode throughout your journey and helps you to reach your destination in time.

© SALES MANTRAS
BY SANDEEP RAVIDUTT SHARMA

Don't expect others to carry your baggage while you are busy closing a deal. Be ready to pitch alone with a warm smile and a strong handshake.

You need to be more aggressive to plan out and acquire a new customer on a regular basis. The business can survive and thrive only when you have new customers lined up continuously and you are able to retain your existing ones with a smile.

© **SALES MANTRAS**
BY SANDEEP RAVIDUTT SHARMA

Be honest about the quality of products you are offering. Let the customer decide whether it is worth buying.

© **SALES MANTRAS**
BY SANDEEP RAVIDUTT SHARMA

Show value for money to the customer if you want to sell.

© **SALES MANTRAS**
BY SANDEEP RAVIDUTT SHARMA

Turn your ideas into innovation with your brilliant efforts.

Never try to score over the customer during your talks especially about the product information unless you are explaining the new features not known to him.

© **SALES MANTRAS**
BY SANDEEP RAVIDUTT SHARMA

A good deal is one where both the buyer and seller wins.

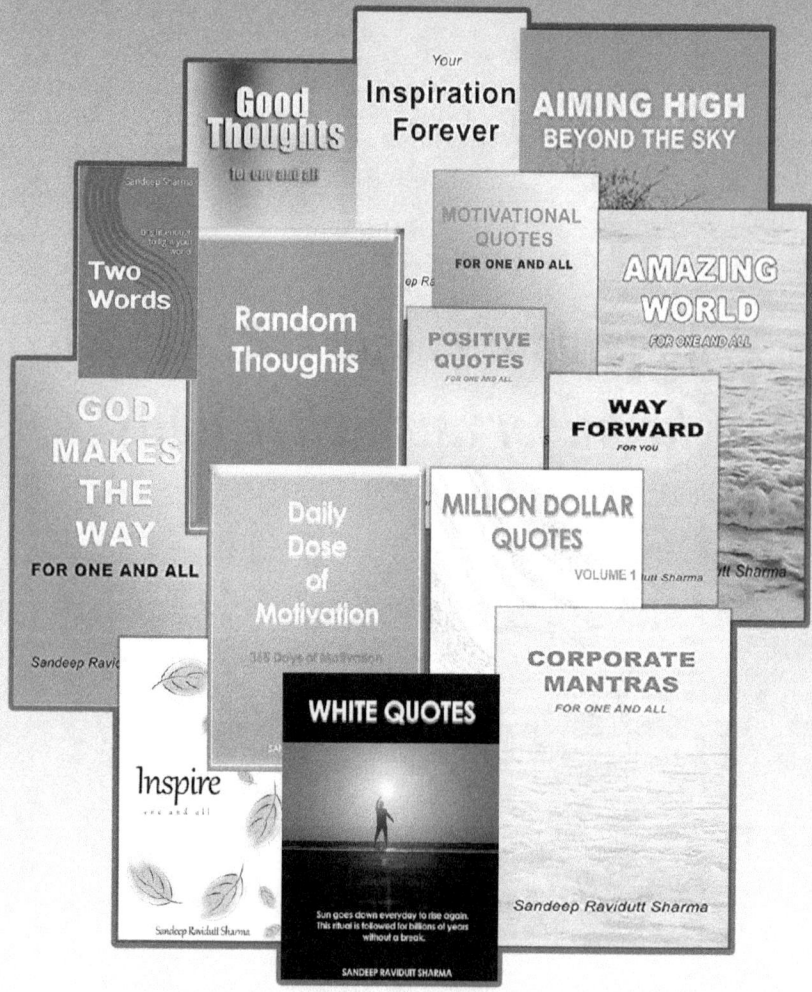

www.ingramcontent.com/pod-product-compliance
Lightning Source LLC
Chambersburg PA
CBHW070803220526
45466CB00002B/531